T0123614

UP TO JESUS

OLIVIA MARIE SOLOMON

WESTBOW
PRESS®
A DIVISION OF THOMAS NELSON
& ZONDERVAN

Copyright © 2024 Olivia Marie Solomon.

All rights reserved. No part of this book may be used or reproduced by any means, graphic, electronic, or mechanical, including photocopying, recording, taping or by any information storage retrieval system without the written permission of the author except in the case of brief quotations embodied in critical articles and reviews.

This book is a work of non-fiction. Unless otherwise noted, the author and the publisher make no explicit guarantees as to the accuracy of the information contained in this book and in some cases, names of people and places have been altered to protect their privacy.

WestBow Press books may be ordered through booksellers or by contacting:

WestBow Press
A Division of Thomas Nelson & Zondervan
1663 Liberty Drive
Bloomington, IN 47403
www.westbowpress.com
844-714-3454

Because of the dynamic nature of the Internet, any web addresses or links contained in this book may have changed since publication and may no longer be valid. The views expressed in this work are solely those of the author and do not necessarily reflect the views of the publisher, and the publisher hereby disclaims any responsibility for them.

Any people depicted in stock imagery provided by Getty Images are models, and such images are being used for illustrative purposes only.
Certain stock imagery © Getty Images.

All Scripture quotations are taken from the King James Version, public domain.

ISBN: 979-8-3850-1287-9 (sc)
ISBN: 979-8-3850-1327-2 (e)

Library of Congress Control Number: 2023922422

Print information available on the last page.

WestBow Press rev. date: 12/29/2023

To anyone seeking encouragement. To anyone looking for direction and a way to turn. To anyone wanting to learn about themselves. To anyone needing a safe place to land. To anyone looking for rest. To anyone wanting to be understood and seen. To anyone fighting a silent battle. To anyone wanting to learn and capture the insurmountable love of their Heavenly Father. My prayer is that through sharing my story, I will share with you tools for navigating life's storms bravely, beautifully, and most importantly, lovingly.

*And this is **love**: that we walk after his commandments. This is the commandment, That, as ye have heard from the beginning, ye should **walk in it**. 2 John 1:6*

CONTENTS

THE CALM BEFORE THE STORM

Well, here we are. Things in life seem to be aligning just as they are meant to be. It's Friday evening. I am on the couch curled up in my "office corner" dressed in half leopard-print pajama pants and half a slightly-weathered sweater. The dog just finished a round of zoomies in the backyard and he's now happy to share his favorite orange ball with me at my feet.

It's looking like a little summer thunderstorm will come through here tonight in beautiful Austin, Texas. The white noise machine gently hums in the background and the air conditioner sets off the occasional cool draft. I usually go for a relaxing cup of hot peppermint tea, but tonight's treat called for a few spoonfuls of cool dairy-free coconut vanilla ice cream. I would say I have a few things on my mind of the past and upcoming, but tonight, and forevermore, I choose peace. I choose these moments of stillness and reflection, filled with immense gratitude for what I have and how far I have come. I choose joy in the unknowing because I know what has been promised to me.

*For I know the thoughts that I think toward you, saith the Lord, thoughts of **peace**, and not of evil, to give you an **expected** end. Jeremiah 29:11*

*For my thoughts are not your thoughts, neither are your ways my ways, saith the Lord. For as the **heavens are higher** than the earth, so are **my ways higher than your ways**, and my thoughts than your thoughts. Isaiah 55:8-9*

THE STORM

L et's just jump into it, shall we? Let's get right to the brass tacks. I'll spill the tea so we can get the clean-up over with. At the end of this month, I am approaching some pretty significant dates. This year marks five years since my father's passing and two years since my ex-husband left; three years apart, very close in date. I also experienced the loss of my beloved dog, Daisy, my grandfather, and the Covid pandemic.

We have all been through some serious tribulations in life as of late. If one thing is for sure, this life is sure to give them. But what I have found is there are so many blessings in the struggle. We don't know why these things happen or how they will turn out, but we do know that things will be okay if we make the best decisions we can through the hard times. It is up to us to choose the next best action to be taken, or inaction, based on the information we are given. Sometimes that decision is just to keep faith alone.

At the end of this month, I have my first scheduled mediation for my pending divorce. It has been two years since my ex-husband and I separated. Now, I want to step out as a testament of my faith in this pivotal time in what appears as a major turning point in my process to speak and claim peace. Before any notable decision has been made by lawyers, mediators, or judges, I am claiming victory. God is in this story. I know The Great I AM has already gone before me and won this battle.

*And we know that in all things work together for good to them that **love God**, to them who are **called according to his purpose**. Romans 8:28*

*See that **none** render evil for evil unto any many; but ever follow which is **good**, both among yourselves, and to **all** men. 1 Thessalonians 5:15*

*I can do all things through **Christ** which **strengtheneth** me. Philipians 4:13*

*Truly my soul **waiteth** upon **God**: from him cometh my salvation. He **only** is my rock and my salvation; he is my **defence**; I shall not be greatly moved. Psalm 62:1-2*

*But they that **wait** upon the **Lord** Shall renew their **strength**; they shall mount up with wings as eagles; They shall run, and not be weary; and they shall walk and not faint. Isaiah 40:31*

ME

Now. The face and heart behind the story. My name is Olivia Marie Solomon. Born as Olivia Marie Colombo, in Long Island, New York and raised in sunny Tampa Bay, Florida. I am 50% Italian. Beach gal. Excellent student. I am five-foot-ten and a half, have long blonde hair, and greenish blue eyes with a sunflower in the middle.

I love animals. I am joyful. I have always been a bit of a social butterfly and have gained many childhood, school, and new friends along the way. I graduated with my Master's Degree in Communication Sciences and Disorders. I work as a Speech-Language Pathologist in skilled nursing facilities primarily with the elderly.

My name means peace, rebellion, peace. My mother is intelligent, an overcomer, and wears her heart on her sleeve. My father and grandfather both served in the military and aspired for righteousness. My grandfather especially led a life rooted in faith, family, and love. My older sister, an artist, and I were raised to be rule-following children and still are. My dad affirmed I am "strong-willed". At our wedding, my father gave my soon to be ex-husband, former NFL player, the warning. The wedding was beautiful, filled with family, love, and joy. Looking back, it was the start of me opening my heart to and trusting God's plans for my life.

I have had my share of naive fun. At twenty, I won a Paris Hilton look-alike contest at a local beach bar and scored a diamond ring. At twenty-seven, I frequented night clubs from Miami to NYC. Back in my hometown, I met a tall, strong blue-eyed funny sweetheart just outside of a dance club. He swept me off my feet all the way to marriage and Austin, TX. I didn't know what I know now.

*Rejoice, O young man, in thy **youth;** and let thy heart cheer thee
in the days of thy youth, and walk in the ways of thine heart,
and in the sight of thine eyes: but know thou, that for all these
things God will bring thee into judgment. Ecclesiastes 11:9*

*He answered and said, Whether he be a sinner or no, I know not: one
thing I know, that, whereas I was **blind,** now I **see**. John 9:25*

*And be **not** conformed to this **world**: but be ye transformed by the renewing of your **mind**, that ye may prove what is that **good**, and **acceptable**, and **perfect**, will of God. Romans 12:2*

ANCHORED

I t is day number two of writing my story. The two years-worth of notes in my phone and mental downloads of memories are pouring down. It rained last night. Not just any rain, but an intense thunderstorm with flash flooding and hail. The storm consisted of momentary rumbles of thunder and crashes of lightning that shook the inner depths of the house. I have always loved thunderstorms growing up in Florida, but these Texas storms are different. Maybe it's the unpredictability of them. It's not what I am used to. Maybe it's because I am alone. But, I have learned to find peace in them. Because I now know that I am truly never alone.

*And he saith unto them, Why are ye fearful, O ye of little **faith**? Then he arose, and rebuked the winds and the sea; and there was a great **calm**. But the men marvelled, saying, What manner of man is this, that even the winds and the sea obey him! Matthew 8:26-27*

WOKE UP IN THE STORM

About three months into my isolation, I experienced an absolutely life-changing moment. First, I began to ask myself questions like: "How did I get here?" "How can life be this hard?" "I thought I did everything I was supposed to do" "What do I do now?" I tried to fix things. I apologized and reached out to those people I thought I may have harmed or hurt along the way. I sat in silence for days on end. Months went by. I could barely make it off the couch nor did I have much desire to. I was being cleansed, purified.

*Come to me, all ye that labour and are heavy laden, and I will give you **rest**. Take my **yoke** upon you and learn of me: for I am **meek** and **lowly** in heart, and ye shall find **rest** unto your souls. For my yoke is **easy,** and my burden is **light**. Matthew 11:28-30*

*The Lord is nigh unto them that are of a **broken heart**, and saveth such as are a contrite spirit. Psalm 34:18*

But then! I am resting on the couch, again, laying on my side facing the back pillows. As I closed my eyes, in efforts to take a nap, I felt a sudden overwhelming physical presence cover me that seemed like what I can only describe as a warm, all encompassing hug. I envisioned I was floating, yet melting into the pillow top of the couch, with an enveloping stillness and quiet. Next, the words rushed into my mind "*You are never alone. I will never forsake you*". In that moment, I was given clarity and the weight of the world was instantly lifted off of me. I fell asleep most soundly and would soon learn, was made new.

As I was with Moses, so I will be with thee: I will
not fail *thee,* ***nor forsake*** *thee. Joshua 1:5*

I will ***never leave*** *thee,* ***nor forsake*** *thee. Hebrews 13:5*

*Then Peter said unto them, **Repent**, and be baptized every one one of you in the name of **Jesus Christ** for the remission of sins, and ye shall receive the gift of the **Holy Ghost**. Acts 2:38*

For a year and a half, I did not know what was happening with my former husband. I felt strongly that it was my position to remain steadfast as a committed wife. I sought couple's counseling and turned inward through personal counseling and much reliance on my faith. I wanted to be supportive, lead with love, and create a safe place for us.

Often when relationships are coming to an end, the lines of communication can be confusing. Seemingly, you are no longer on the same wavelength. Our last visit reminded me of the sweet and gentle man I married, and how long I had missed this person, but deep down I knew this chapter was closing. I knew it was time to move forward in my truth. I needed wise counsel, guidance, and support. But above all, God would guide me through.

*I can do all things through **Christ** which*
***strengtheneth** me. Philippians 4:13*

*Then said Jesus, Father, **forgive them**; for they*
do not know what they do. Luke 23:34

*And he said to them all: If any man will come after me, let him **deny himself**, and take up his **cross daily**, and **follow me** . Luke 9:23*

*And when ye stand praying, if ye have ought against any: that your Father also which is in heaven may **forgive** you your trespasses. Mark 11:25*

*And therefore will the Lord **wait**, that he may be **gracious** unto you, and therefore will he be exalted, that he may have **mercy** upon you: for the Lord is a God of **judgment**: blessed are all they that **wait** for him. Isaiah 30:18*

*Now therefore hearken unto me, O ye children: for blessed are they that **keep my ways**. Hear instruction, and be wise, and refuse it not. Proverbs 8:32-33*

THE CLEANUP

Mind you, I had never really read the Bible. I did not have scripture memorized. I had been ministered to throughout my life by some amazing mentors in Christ, but that moment in my living room was without a doubt a supernatural experience from God. Following that experience, God continued to speak to me in my solitude that led to my ultimate healing, step by step. He guided me to start nourishing myself with healthy food and drink. Plenty of rest continued to be essential. Light exercise through stretching and easy body movements added to my strength. Eventually, I was able to enjoy more advanced exercises again.

Next, God brought me outside to remind me of His Presence in nature and beauty. He showed me perfectly painted sunsets, uniquely woven trails, and refreshing streams of water. He guided me to His Word in a daily devotional, faith-based books, and, soon, the Bible. I learned about His heart and the importance of spending time with Him. God led me back to work which eventually led me to see His Presence most magnificently in other people.

I know God has been pursuing me my entire life, but it has been up to this particular point that I was able to put it all together. I am so sure of His divine intervention and healing of my heart that I want to share it with you. Because I am telling you, in this mess, I have been blessed, and there is only one way I am here as I am today, and it is because of Jesus.

Ask, and it shall be ***given*** you; ***seek*** and ye shall ***find***; ***knock,*** and it shall be ***opened*** unto you. *Matthew 7:7*

*My sheep **hear** my voice, I **know** them, and they **follow** me. John 10:27*

Jesus *saith unto him, I am the **way,** the **truth,** and the **life:** no man cometh unto the **Father,** but by me. John 14:6*

*The Lord is my shepherd; I shall not want. He maketh me to lie down in **green pastures**: he leadeth me beside the **still waters**. He **restoreth** my soul: he leadeth me in the paths of righteousness for his name's sake. Psalm 23:1-3*

*Surely **goodness** and **mercy** shall follow me all the days of my life: and I will dwell in the **house** of the **Lord forever**. Psalm 23:6*

THE CLEANUP CREW

Throughout my life I have been blessed with a number of spiritual mentors that spoke truth and life over me. I am grateful for my grandfather, "Papa", who lived a life dedicated to service and the love of all people for 102 years. He would tell me I have "the light in me". I now know he was speaking of the light of Christ.

In my recent storms, God showed up incredibly through doctors, counselors, family, and friends. My doctors lent a listening ear, encouragement, and gave me tools to get to long-lasting better health. Christian counselors provided me with the application of God's Word to my current "life storms" and reminded me of the unfailing hope of His promises. Endless conversations, books, reading the Bible, and prayer carried me through. My family remained loyal by my side and grew with me in my faith walk. Old friends checked in on me and reminded me of a child-like joy. New friends through church and women's groups gave me a safe place to share my story and walk with God in community.

I learned of the undeniable power of God's love for me and that He is fervently after my heart. I learned that I was chosen and saved by His grace. God even made Himself most notably obvious through patients I would visit with at work and strangers alike. These divine appointments deserve an explanation in great, illuminating detail.

*O give **thanks** unto the Lord, for he is **good**: for
his mercy endureth **forever**. Psalm 107:1*

*Which doeth **great** things and unsearchable;
marvelous things without number. Job 5:9*

*For by **grace** are ye **saved** by **faith**; and that not of yourselves: it is a **gift of God**. Ephesians 2:8-9*

HE LOVES ME

Back at work, I found great respite starting my day off down in the memory care center as they often had group activities for the seniors. On this day, one of my co-workers had a group gathered around as she played the classical piano. A caretaker came to join the group with one of my favorite patients, J, who was memory impaired and mostly nonverbal. She sat down with J and closed her eyes as the group sang *Amazing Grace*. As soon as I saw the caregiver Natalie, I felt a tug to reach out to her. I watched her enjoy the music and waved to her, welcoming her to the group. Natalie and J rocked back and forth to the music, ever so peacefully.

After the music, the residents gathered in the dining room for dinner. I looked over to Natalie sitting with J at the table, this time, now holding a Bible. I immediately bee-lined my way over to her. I said, "Is that your Bible?" "Do you read that to her?" As I was looking closer I could see the Bible was well-read with many colorful Post-It notes in it, Natalie clinging to it tightly. Natalie said, "Yes, this is my lifeline" "I read it to her sometimes too". I said "That is wonderful!" Then I asked "How long have you been reading the Bible?" Natalie shared her testimony of ten years ago. She said she was in the bathtub at her lowest point when the Holy Spirit came and saved her. I thanked her for bravely sharing her story. I told her that I had been going through some hard things lately and that I was really leaning on my faith.

In that incredible moment, Natalie turned right toward me as her piercing blue eyes made direct and intense contact with mine and said "It is your husband isn't it?" Natalie embraced my hands and hugged me tightly and began to pray. She spoke in the Spirit language. She rocked me back and forth and said "God loves you so much!" The patient J, reached out to me grabbing for my hands and said "Have I told you how much I love you lately? "I love you so much!"

An intense hot flash came over my entire body and tears came rushing down as I felt an immediate sense of relief. Natalie said when you cry, it is confirmation that God is with you. She said, "this is your confirmation from God that everything is going to be okay". She said, "I don't know what your husband is dealing with right now, but he will be okay." "As a wife you have to be strong". The moment froze in time and felt like it lasted forever. I could eventually hear my coworker speaking to another resident in the background. Natalie asked if I had a support group or someone to talk to at church. She said to read Scripture and speak it aloud for God and others to hear. So that's exactly what I did.

*Go ye therefore and **teach** all nations, **baptizing** them in the name of the **Father,** and of the **Son**, and of the **Holy Ghost**. Matthew 28:19*

***Charity suffereth long**, and is **kind**, charity envieth not: charity vaunteth not itself, is not puffed up, Doth not behave itself unseemly, seeketh not her own, is not easily provoked, thinketh no evil; Rejoiceth not in iniquity, but rejoiceth in the **truth**; Beareth all things, believeth all things, hopeth all things, endureth all things. 1 Corinthians 13:4-7*

MY FRIEND

Hello, me again. It's day three writing my story. The rain has ceased for a few hours and there is sun shining through the clouds. The journey through my healing has been much like this. Each day I'd wake up and face the new realities and thoughts to mull through. I'd get in prayer, spend time reading, and gradually get enough courage and focus to head into work. Many notable days at the nursing home I was able to visit with my patient M.

A mother of seven, grandmother of 13, and great-grandmother of countless more, M was cherished by her loving family. She knew many people in the community as M and her husband had lived there for many years. M was a newer widow but continued her journey in life with strength and confidence. After completing her course in cognitive therapy, I would occasionally check on M just to see how she was doing. Her sea-blue eyes, perfectly put-together knit sweater assemblages, and her four-foot tall stature was a sweet reminder of security and order to me.

Christmas came and shortly into the new year, M's health began to decline. First, at 87 years-young she battled Covid and persevered through. Her walking became more difficult and falling became a significant risk. The nursing staff and family provided options to keep her safe including a medical alert system she could wear in case of an emergency. I wanted to do something nice to keep her spirit up so I ordered M a little special something that would shortly arrive in the mail. M began to have trouble eating and her appetite became poor, so we found that chocolate milkshakes by the spoon did the job. One day we were able to enjoy looking over a photo album one of her sons brought while learning about her heritage and old family trips, of course, complemented by the chocolate milkshake.

Soon, M's special gift arrived: a beautiful long silver chain necklace with royal blue resin and glass crystal beads. I figured it would be a functional and tasteful way she could wear her medical alert system. I showed M the new jewelry accessory and placed it around her head ever so gently. I told her "you are loved".

The weekend went by and I returned to work the following Monday. I was running around seeing some other patients on my schedule, when I saw a familiar face of a middle-aged woman walking down the hall. I more or less walked right to her and as we greeted each other I noticed her sweet, endearing ocean water-colored blue eyes. It was one of M's daughters, one which I had not yet met.

I quickly realized who she was. She explained that she was thanking the staff for what good care her mother received at the facility. The night before coming into work I had a feeling M would soon pass away. All in that moment, my mind sorted all of what was happening and as I looked down I saw a beautiful silver and blue beaded chain necklace around M's daughter's neck. I smiled and shed some tears as she proceeded to show me the necklace and say, "I saw this on my mom the other night and I asked her where she got it. M's reply, "from my friend".

*Who can find a **virtuous** woman? for her price
is far above **rubies**. Proverbs 31:10*

*Give her of the fruit of her hands; and let her own
works **praise** her in the gates. Proverbs 31:31*

RECENE

My Goldendoodle dog, Jock, has been by my side since the day I took him home. On the days I needed rest most of the time, he rested with me. In moments of panic, he calmed me. At my lowest, when I would take him outside, I would sit on the corner of the deck with my head collapsed in my hands. Eventually, I would feel the sun and "look up". Those simple moments of just being still and focusing on the present grew to be my most cherished moments. I realized God was showing up for me through Jock, in unconditional love. What a precious gift from Heaven he is.

I was reminded of the beauty of God's creation when my father passed away. I thought if my dad was a bird, he would be a blue jay. Not just because of his "baby blues", but because of the J in his first name ("Julius"). My dad was also my fearless protector. While he was in the hospital, I prayed for a sign from God that everything would be okay. Let me tell you, blue jays came to my backyard in numbers! But mainly the one big ol' blue jay that came right up to my sliding glass door, standing on the ground, looking straight at me as soon as the prayer formed in my mind. I laughed and cried in awe about how obvious it was that He is real!

More fun times in nature meant more fun times through God instances. Jock fits his name well and he gave me something to chase after and run with. On another park outing, dogs could be off leash, so I decided to start working on it with him. Jock did really well and ran around with some other dogs in groups. His favorite two were named Cowboy and Bandit. Naturally, as time went on, the dogs got a little rebellious and ran to the next park over.

As we were wrapping up our time, Jock wandered away for one more adventure. I saw him heading toward a man laying in the grass on a blanket under a tree. In Austin culture, this is just the laid back, get with nature, and enjoy your afternoon kinda way. Jock made his way over to the man pretty quickly and before I knew it, he was cuddling the man, rubbing his head against his and rolling over him. As I got close, I realized the man was sleeping. Not only this, he was frail, had long unkempt hair, and had sparing amounts of stale bread around him. He was homeless.

I apologized to the man for my dog coming over unexpectedly and invading his space. I explained, "he just loves". Suddenly, the man looked at me, through his sharp blue eyes, and said intently "it's all about you". It wasn't so much about what he said that day, but it was about the feeling it left me with. Something extraordinary in that moment felt peaceful and filled with compassion as if he was explaining I did not need to apologize, but to receive love and grace as things are. This is God's love.

*For God so **loved** the world, that he gave his only begotten **Son**, that whosoever **believeth** in him should not perish, but have **everlasting life**. John 3:16*

*And to **love** him with all the **heart**, and with all the **understanding**, and with all the **soul,** and with all the **strength**, and to **love his neighbour** as himself, is more than all whole burnt offerings and sacrifices. Mark 12:33*

Another Earth angel came to me when I ventured out on my first trip away from home since my healing journey. Her name was Maria and I met her on the plane ride back from San Francisco to Austin during Holy Week. Maria, with her long curly brown hair, sun-kissed highlights, and giddy personality, welcomed me into her row to sit in the empty seat next to her. I felt a "tug" to settle in that seat as well.

Being that it was my return trip, I was pretty tuckered out and prepared to close my eyes and catch some rest. About fifteen minutes into the flight, Maria and I jumped right into conversation that would soon continue nonstop for the remainder of the three and a half hour long flight. I learned that Maria was a single mother of a teenage son and a teacher of many sorts. She shared her story of relationship hardships with me and I shared mine. We exchanged comfort and support to each other, including tears.

Maria explained her faith journey to me in ways I could truly understand and relate to. In one instance, she explained it as we are all given an "assignment" while here on Earth. Our assignment allows us to grow in character and become closer to God in Heaven. When I asked how I would know if I am doing okay, she exclaimed, "you are talking about Jesus during Holy Week, you are there!" Maria also noted that not everyone will be part of your story, but God will place those in your path that are meant to be part of His plan for you, and theirs. Maria was definitely one of those important people for me.

Day four of writing my story. There is no rain today, yet. As I am reliving a lot of my faith journey, my faith is strengthened. Per the course, God is continuing to show more of Himself to me, furthering my understanding and relationship with Him. I am reassured at how far I have come. It is still cloudy today, the rain will come again, so the storm is not quite over. But I wouldn't want to be anywhere else in my life or out of this storm because I have contentment. I have clarity. I have peace. I have hope. I have love.

LOVE

L ove is what God has shown me. I have learned that God is love. Through the amazing eye-opening experiences in nature, people, and circumstances, I have seen God's love. I have felt God's love, supernaturally and undeniably. I have learned that God is seeking you, actively pursuing each and everyone of us, we only need to receive, to reply. Just like any other human relationship, it starts with a knowing, a meeting if you will, and the bond grows over time. If we spend time with a person, we get to know them.

God is the one person that is all things: He is gentle, humble, compassionate, funny, bold, helpful, friendly, strong, unchanging, omnipotent, omnipresent, Almighty and the list goes on. He experiences all of the emotions we do, but He is made perfect in love. As we learn to know Him, we will want to grow in our character to be like Him. The desire of God's heart is for our heart to be like His heart. That is, God's desires will become our desires and our will will align with His will. The closer in intimacy we are with our Heavenly Father, our heart (body), mind, and soul will be renewed and restored. We will be made brand new.

*Ye are of God, **little children**, and have **overcome** them, because **greater is He** that is in you than he that is in the world. 1 John 4:4*

*We **love** him, because he first loved us. 1 John 4:19*

*Charity suffereth long, and is **kind;** charity envieth not; charity vaunteth not itself, is not puffed up; doth not behave itself unseemly, seeketh not her own, is not easily provoked, thinketh no evil; rejoiceth not in iniquity, but **rejoiceth** in the **truth;** **beareth** all things, **believeth** all things, **hopeth** all things, **endureth** all things. 1 Corinthians 13:1-7*

NEW ME

Being in a community with other Believers allowed me to get stronger in my faith walk. I prayed that the Lord would guide me every step of the way and He did just that. I did a lot of independent study to learn about God. I read stacks of books that were based around scripture. Reading the Bible itself has been the most profound tool I have found in my life. At first, I decided it was best to read it aloud, speaking the words, clearly and precisely.

During these times, I would get moments of clarity, strength, and direction in what next steps to take in my personal relationships, work, and other life matters. Eventually, I really began to comprehend God's Word and His message became so clear to me through the help of the Holy Spirit. I was guided to join a church community where I could learn more about the gospel and share in faith stories. I became pretty active in a women's group and Bible study that met once or twice a week. I eventually became a greeter for the Sunday church service. After about six months, I felt God led me to get baptized as an adult and to display my commitment and invigorated faith in the Lord to the Lord. I repented of my sins and accepted Jesus Christ as my Lord and Savior.

*Then Peter said unto them, **Repent**, and be baptized every one of you in the name of Jesus Christ for the remission of sins, and ye shall receive the gift of the **Holy Ghost**. Acts 2:38*

*Jesus answered, Verily, verily, I say unto thee, Except a man be **born of water** and of the **Spirit**, he cannot enter into the **kingdom of God**. John 3:5*

*Therefore, if any man be in **Christ**, he is a **new creature**: old things are passed away; behold, all things are **become new.** 2 Corinthians 5:17*

*That if thou shalt confess with thy mouth the Lord Jesus, and shalt believe in thine heart that God hath raised him from the dead, thou shalt be saved. For with the **heart** man believeth unto righteousness; and with the **mouth** confession is made unto salvation. Romans 10:9-10*

I was reborn. In the deepest moments of reflection, when I laid in isolation at my lowest, allowing the peeling and pruning of the thoughts and conceptions I had picked up in my life, is when the most clarity came. It's when I let go of the ideas that gave me comfort of "who I was" and the "identity I had formed", to stop leaning on my own understanding and believing in the impossible. I started believing in God's Word. I came to the end of myself. I died to myself. I laid it all down at the cross. I remained in faith. I repented of my sins. I was saved by God's mercy and grace. I was delivered. I was redeemed. I was restored. I have been made whole.

> *Trust in the Lord with all thine **heart**; and lean not unto thine own understanding. In all thy ways **acknowledge** him, and he shall **direct thy paths**. Proverbs 3:5-6*

> *For if ye live after the flesh, ye shall die; but if ye through the **Spirit** do mortify the deeds of the body, ye shall **live.** Romans: 8:13*

*For whosoever will **save** his life shall lose it; but whosoever shall lose his life for my sake and the gospel's, the same shall **save** it. Mark 8:35*

*O generation of vipers, how can ye, being evil, speak good things? For out of abundance of the **heart** the mouth speaketh. Matthew 12:34*

*Therefore leaving the principles of the doctrine of Christ, let us go on unto **perfection**; not laying again the foundation of repentance from dead works, and of faith toward God, Hebrews 6:1*

I am a new creation in Christ Jesus. My mind, heart, and spirit have been renewed. Through Christ, I know that I am loved beyond comprehension. And you are too. I know He created me in His image and I am perfectly made. I am made exactly how He planned it from the beginning of time. I have learned to love myself for who I am, unfiltered. Putting on the armor of God, fighting off and unlearning every mistruth or lie spoken over me has ensured my victory. And He has this same hope for all of His children. His love is unconditional and unwavering.

HOPE IN THE MUD

This world has placed unrealistic and upside down truths on society that do not align with how we were purposed. I share my story because I *know* there is a real enemy of darkness and evil spiritual principalities and powers. As a result, seducing spirits and doctrines of demons relentlessly attempt to wrongly influence our thinking by deception and confusion. Satan will use power, control, and manipulation of our thoughts to steer us away from God's perfect love, plans, and purposes for our lives. He will attack our spirit, soul, or body, or all three.

Satan's goal is to cultivate and trap us in feelings of abandonment, loss, failure, grief, hurt, disappointment, pain, rejection, betrayal, guilt, shame, condemnation, sickness, lack, inferiority, laziness, loneliness, fear, anxiety, depression, worry, doubt, sadness, confusion, worthlessness (unworthiness), helplessness, hopelessness, unbelief, envy, anger, greed, pride, entitlement, lust, idolatry, etc. He lures us into his mud with the temptation of temporary and nonproductive solutions of what we are experiencing on the inside. And the thing is, he places those seeds of negative thoughts in us in the first place! Anything that does not align with God's truths of who He says we are (LOVED, VALUED, ONE OF A KIND, and FREE), is not of God. If not held captive, these thoughts will lead our lives (and lead us away from God's just and perfect will for us).

Deeply-rooted thoughts become beliefs, which occur without conscious thinking. Anything we come into agreement with, knowingly or unknowingly, in our hearts and minds outside of God's truths is a sin. In this life on Earth we are given a choice: we can have eternity with our loving Father in Heaven or we can have an eternal absence from Him. We can choose to end the war right here and right now. God's love will break the chains releasing you into freedom. You need only to wholeheartedly trust Him and willingly give Him your burdens. Guard your hearts and minds in Christ Jesus with everything you have as if your life depends on it. Because it does. *Receive His love wholeheartedly.* God has so much for you beyond your wildest dreams.

HOLY ROLY

Be not deceived: neither fornicators, nor idolaters, nor adulterers, nor effeminate, nor abusers of themselves with mankind, nor thieves, nor covetous, nor drunkards, nor revilers, nor extortioners, shall inherit the kingdom of God. 1 Corinthians 6:9-10

Now the works of the flesh are made manifest, which are these; Adultery, fornication, uncleanness, lasciviousness, idolatry, witchcraft, hatred, variance, emulations, wrath, strife, seditions, heresies, envyings, murders, drunkenness, revellings, and such like: of the which I tell you before, as I have also told you in time past, that they which do such things shall not inherit the kingdom of God. Galatians 5:19-21

These six things doth the LORD hate: yea, seven are an abomination unto him: A proud look, a lying tongue, and hands that shed innocent blood, An heart that deviseth wicked imaginations, feet that be swift in running to mischief, A false witness that speaketh lies, and he that soweth discord among brethren. Proverbs 6:16-19

Where there is dark, there is always light and where there is light, there is darkness lurking around the corner. It started at the beginning of time with Adam and Eve (and that pesky serpent), and, well, times are more urgent than ever before. We are living in a fallen world. We must be aware of the Devil's schemes in order to a) *know* to fight it and b) how to fight it. And that is, with God's Word and truths planted firmly in our hearts and minds. We are made strong in Him.

It is not something that is so obvious to the untrained eye or the person who seeks "comfort", complacency, or status quo. It's not going to come to those who "don't want to rock the boat". It is hidden in what unfortunately society has made "the normal". But for anyone who starts to question why things are the way they are in this world and what needs to be done differently, the truth can be revealed.

You can live a holy life and walk in purity. *Be ye holy, for I am holy. 1 Peter 1:16.* It's something much deeper that is in our hearts if we are willing to listen. It's a battle for our souls. It's spiritual warfare. It's good versus evil. Mercifully, the battle has already been won by our almighty Lord, Jesus Christ. He is the savior of hearts. We can have more for our families and generations to come if we just seek Him.

*The thief cometh not, but for to **steal**, and to*
***kill**, and to **destroy**: John 10:10*

*But even the very hairs of your head are all numbered. **Fear not***
therefore: ye are of more value than many sparrows. Luke 12:7

*Finally, my brethren, be **strong** in the Lord, and in the **power** of*
*his might. Put on the whole **armour of God**, that ye may be able*
to stand against the wiles of the devil. For we wrestle not against
principalities, against powers, against the rulers of darkness of this
world, against spiritual wickedness in high places. Ephesians 6:10-12

*Wherefore take unto you the **whole armor of God**, that ye may be able to*
*withstand in the evil day, and having done all, **to stand**. Stand therefore,*
*having your loins girt about with **truth**, and having on the breastplate of*
***righteousness**; And your feet shod with the preparation of the gospel of*
***peace**; Above all, taking the shield of **faith**, wherewith ye shall be able to*
*quench all the fiery darts of the wicked. And take the helmet of **salvation**,*
*and the sword of the **Spirit**, which is the **word of God: Praying always***
*with all prayer and supplication in the **Spirit**, and watching thereunto*
*with all **perseverance** and supplication for all saints; Ephesians 6:13-18*

(For the weapons of our warfare are not carnal, but mighty through
*God to the **pulling down of strongholds**;) 2 Corinthians 10:4*

*Seeing then that all these things shall be dissolved, what manner of persons ought ye to be in all **holy** conversation and **godliness**. 2 Peter 3:11*

*And one cried unto another, and said, **Holy**, **holy**, **holy**, is the **Lord of hosts**: the whole earth is full of **his glory**. Isaiah 6:3*

*There hath no **temptation** taken you but such as is common to man: but God is faithful, who will not suffer you to be tempted above that ye are able; but will with the temptation also make a way to **escape**, that ye may be able to bear it. 1 Corinthians 10:13*

*Thou wilt keep him in **perfect peace**, whose **mind** is stayed on thee: because he trusteth in thee. Isaiah 26:3*

*If the **Son** therefore shall make you **free**, ye shall be **free indeed**. John 8:36*

THE TREE

t is day number five of writing my story. The rain came a little during the day but just for a brief moment and enough to leave its wet evidence on the sidewalks. I noticed my plants are growing quickly, sprouting up new buds out from underneath the winter freeze. Some plants are recognizably the same plant from last season with new bright green stems and leaves, others with blooming flowers of arrays of color, and some are just weeds.

For the good fruit to bear, the right conditions were set for the harvest. Old, rotten tree parts pruned and removed, new soil, nutrients, time, water, sunshine, and faith allowed new creation to form. Similar to our hearts, unproductive and damaged things of the past must be uprooted and replaced with nourishment. In learning who God is, He gently replaces the parts of ourselves that are angry, sad, bitter, anxious, confused, etc and replaces those areas with His perfect truths. His perfect truths allow good, healthy roots; a tree that produces good, healthy fruits. As we walk with the Lord, our character grows to be like Jesus': in *love, joy, peace, longsuffering, gentleness, goodness, faith, meekness, temperance. Galatians 5:22-23*

With these character traits, there is no room for the enemy. Spiritual discernment is gained in which the Believer is able to understand or know something through the power of the Spirit. Discernment is for our protection and revelation is in alignment with God's love for us. Most vitally, discernment allows us to distinguish God's voice from others. Again, if we love Him, we would want to follow Him, heed to His advice, and honor His ways. God's commandments: *To love the Lord your God, and to serve Him with all your heart and with all your soul. Deuteronomy 11:13*

Additionally, God's love languages can be found in *The Ten Commandments: Thou shalt have no other gods before me. Thou shalt not take the name of the Lord thy God in vain. Remembereth the **sabbath day**, to* *keep it holy. Honor thy father and thy mother. Thou shalt not kill. Thou shalt not commit adultery. Thou shalt not steal. Thou shalt not bear false witness against thy neighbour. Thou shalt not covet thy neighbour's house, thou shalt not covet thy neighbour's wife, nor his manservant, nor his maidservant, nor his ox, nor his ass, nor any thing that is thy neighbour's. Exodus 20:17*

*The thief cometh not, but for to steal and to kill, and to destroy: I am come that they might have **life**, and that they might have it more **abundantly**. John 10:10*

*There is no fear in love; but **perfect love** casteth out fear. 1 John 4:18*

*And God said, Let the Earth bring forth grass, the herb yielding seed, and the fruit tree yielding fruit after his kind, **whose seed is in itself**, upon the earth: and it was so. Genesis 1:11*

*Abide in me, and I in you. As the **branch** cannot bear **fruit** of itself, except it abide in the **vine**; no more can ye, except ye abide in me. I am the vine, ye are the branches: He that abideth in me, and I in him, the same bringeth forth much fruit: for without me ye can do nothing. John 15:4-5*

*__I in them, and thou in me__, that they may be made **perfect in one**, and that the world may know that **thou hast sent me, and hast loved them, as thou hast loved Me**. John 17:23*

*But the fruit of the Spirit is **love, joy, peace, longsuffering, kindness, gentleness, goodness, faith, meekness, temperance**: against such there is no law. Galatians 5:22-23*

*And, behold, **I** come quickly; and my **reward** is with me, to give **every man according as his** work shall be. Revelation 22:12*

*Be not deceived; God is not mocked: for whatsoever a man **soweth**, that shall he also **reap**. For he that soweth to his flesh shall of the flesh reap corruption; but he that soweth to the **Spirit** shall of the **Spirit** reap life everlasting. And let us not be weary in well doing: for in due season we shall reap, if we faint not. As we have therefore opportunity, let us do good unto all men, especially unto them who are of the household of faith. Galatians 6:7-10*

SERVICE

Early on in my faith journey, I knew the importance of serving others for the Lord. God pursued me in my solitude, but also made His Presence evident to me as I served others. It's as if nothing made Him more happy than to provide a beautiful exchange of love and His blessings between multiples of His children at the same time. And usually it is in our suffering where God uses us most greatly to help others, to show His glory. We only need to lean into the pain and push through it with God in our purpose. *And he said unto me, My grace is sufficient for thee: for my **strength** is made perfect in weakness. 2 Corinthians 12:9*

It always gave me great joy to help others, but now I have a more clear purpose and guide in what I am being used for. As I became more filled up with God's perfect love, I was able to pour into others. I learned that one of my God-given gifts is wisdom. Not of my own, but His wisdom through me.

Other spiritual gifts include teachers, healers, helpers, and administrators. We are not limited to one of these spiritual gifts, but can demonstrate a number of them. As a new friend at work, B, stated "we all have a piece or pieces of the puzzle". Everyone's part is needed. *For as the body is one and has many members, but all the members of that one body, being many, are one body, so also is Christ. 1 Corinthians 12:12.* Asking for God's will over my own in my life has been the ultimate game-changer.

I know that whatever God has planned is the best plan for me and I only need to be obedient to His plan. Daily, in every area of my life, from moment to moment, I say, "God, please show me". The Holy Spirit leads me. In times of uncertainty, I chose "the next best thing" in His eyes. Love God with all of your heart. Love your neighbor. Do what is good, always. Walk holy and be obedient to His commands.

*Now there are diversities of **gifts**, but the same **Spirit**. 1 Corinthians 12:4*

*But the manifestation of the Spirit is given to every man to profit withal. For to one is given by the Spirit the word of **wisdom**; to another the word of **knowledge** by the same Spirit; To another **faith** by the same Spirit; to another the gifts of **healing** by the same Spirit;To another the working of **miracles**; to another **prophecy**; to another **discerning** of spirits; to another divers kinds of **tongues**; to another the **interpretation** of tongues. 1 Corinthians 12:7-10*

*Not by might, nor by power, but by my **spirit**, saith the LORD of hosts. Zechariah 4:6*

*And God hath set some in the church: first **apostles**, secondly **prophets**, thirdly **teachers**, after that **miracle workers**, then those with gifts of **healing**, **helpers**, **administrators**, and those with **diversity of tongues.** 1 Corinthians 12:28*

*And he gave some, **apostles**; and some, **prophets;** and some, **evangelists**; and some, **pastors** and **teachers**. Ephesians 4:11*

*And it shall come to pass, if ye shall hearken diligently unto my **commandments** which I command you this day, to love the Lord your God and to **serve** Him with all your **heart** and with all your **soul,** Deuteronomy 11:13*

COMMUNITY

I t is day six of my writing journey. No rain. Just calm. Percentages are low for any showers and there is a stillness settling into this week-long rain forecast. I am trusting the process. I am leaning into it and feeling grounded. I have faith that this weather will soon pass, and there is much security and beauty in the uncertainty.

Today, I reflect on how blessed I have been by the receiving of community. God led me to people in which He continued to work in me, around me, through me, and through others. I learned the importance of having other Believers in your life to lift you up and remind you of God's truths and His promises. Together, we can remain steadfast in breaking the chains of shame, helplessness, fear, grief, condemnation, confusion, distractions, and guilt to be replaced with God's perfect love. I learned to walk by faith and not by sight. *Now faith is the substance of things hoped for, the evidence of things not seen. Hebrews 11:1*

*And let us consider one another to provoke unto **love** and to **good** **works**, not forsaking the assembling of ourselves **together**, as is the manner of some, but **exhorting** one another, and so much the more as ye see the day approaching. Hebrews 10:24-25*

*Behold, how good and how pleasant it is For brethren to dwell **together** in **unity**! Psalm 133:1*

*And the **peace** of God, which passeth all understanding, shall keep your **hearts** and **minds** through Christ Jesus. Philippians 4:7*

*And concerning the **tithe** of the herd, or of the flock, even of whatsoever passeth under the rod, the tenth shall be holy unto the Lord. Leviticus 27:32*

PRAYER

Prayer is an integral part of your relationship with God. It is a direct communication of your heart's desires, concerns, needs, and requests. It is a telephone call to God. It is a two way text message. It is a love letter. It is your way of communicating to the Creator of the Universe.

Words hold power and when you speak them aloud, your Creator hears. When speaking your prayers aloud, there is intention put behind what you say. Do not think of this as selfish, for what kind of relationship would you have with any person that you did not speak with? God speaks to us through His Word and Holy Spirit, and we can listen. We also speak and communicate back to Him. It's a reciprocal relationship of giving and receiving. It is intimacy. Ask God anything, tell Him all of your worries and concerns. Leave it all at His feet. Journal, draw, paint, create, or just be still. When you have no words, God hears the meditations of your heart. Pray in the *Spirit*. Inhale breath of life, exhale breath of life.

Pray for your circumstances, pray for others' circumstances, pray for your family, pray for your friends, pray for forgiveness, pray to forgive others. Pray that you learn who you are in God's image and that your heart be aligned with His plan for your life. Pray your heart and mind becomes like His. Pray to remove anything in your heart that is not of Him. Break agreement with any evil spirit coming against you or your family. Repent of your sins. My most frequent prayer is Father, your will, not mine. There is power in prayer. Prayer is the answer.

After this manner therefore pray ye: ***Our Father who art in heaven, Hallowed be Thy name. Thy kingdom come, Thy will be done in earth as it is in heaven. Give us this day our daily bread. And forgive us our debts, as we forgive our debtors. Lead us not into temptation, but deliver us from evil: For thine is the kingdom, and the power, and the glory, for ever. Amen.*** *Matthew 6:9-13*

*Watch ye and pray, lest ye enter into temptation. The **Spirit** is truly **ready,** but the flesh is weak. Mark 14:38*

*And he said unto them, This kind can come forth by nothing, but by **prayer** and **fasting.** Mark 9:29*

*And they were all filled with the Holy Ghost, and began to speak with other tongues, as the **Spirit** gave them utterance. Acts 2:4*

*Now when this was noised abroad, the multitude came **together**, and were confounded, because that every man heard them speak in his own **language**. Acts 2:6*

***Praying always** with all prayer and supplication in the Spirit, and watching thereunto with all **perseverance** and supplication for all saints; Ephesians 6:18*

WORSHIP AND PRAISE

Hello, day number seven of my writing journey. It is raining again, with much of a downpour and occasional thunder. I am reminded to *Count it all joy when ye fall into divers temptations; Knowing this, that the trying of your faith worketh patience. James 1:2-3.* I remember God's *strength being made perfect in weakness. 2 Corinthians 12:9.* I am happy to *Make a joyful noise unto the Lord, all ye lands. Serve the Lord with gladness: come before His presence with singing. Psalm 100:1-2*

Music (singing, dancing, instrumental) has always been a big part of my life and passed down through generations. It is the love language I am happy to share with my father, grandfather, and Heavenly Father. The Lord honors our praise because it glorifies Him in Heaven. Worship allows us to step into His Presence. There is peace in His Presence.

Worship music includes Scripture of God's Word which makes it so powerful. It allows us another way to speak fruitful messages and fill up on God's promises. As we know, our words and thoughts hold power. God spoke the world into existence. That same power lives within us through Him.

As I am growing back into my own, I am singing and dancing again; but this time with the intention of praising God and bringing Him glory. I am singing and dancing in worship by myself, at church, at work, and with friends. I am praising God through the highs and the lows. I have seen the tremendous benefits of encouraging others to join in worship as it collectively heals our hearts. The Lord's joy is absolutely contagious. We were made to worship.

Come join the party and joyous celebration of praise! Raise your hands to the sky and praise Him. Selah! It's a dance party with Jesus. Your Heavenly Father basks in your praise.

*Hear, O ye kings; give ear, O ye princes; I, even I, will **sing** unto the Lord; I will **sing praise** to the Lord God of Israel. Judges 5:3*

*And all the people saw the cloudy pillar stand at the tabernacle door; and all the people rose up and **worshipped**, every man in his tent door. Exodus 33:10*

*And the man **bowed down** his head, and*
***worshipped** the Lord. Genesis 24:26*

*I will **praise** You, O Lord, with my whole heart; I will tell of*
*all Your marvelous works. I will be glad and **rejoice** in You;I*
*will **sing praise** to Your name, O Most High. Psalm 9:1-2*

***Praise** Him with the sound of the trumpet: praise*
Him with the psaltery and harp. Psalm 150:3

PRINCESS

I t is day eight of my writing. The sun is out! There is joy in the morning! The storm has, indeed, passed. I have been persevering through reliving the details of my "storm" to share with you, and it has resulted in a number of emotions over the past week (now turned to months). There's been some heaviness, mixed with new/ revealed perspectives, but most importantly, hope remains.

I know this is a necessary part of going through the process of healing, leaning into the pain. But I know with certainty, I do not have to stay there. The wounds will eventually heal completely, and I will be made stronger. I am stronger. I am loved. I know who I am and who I am becoming in Christ. I am His beloved.

God has used my pain to grow closer in relationship with Him. In Him, there is peace and clarity, a deep-knowing that He will unveil the plans He has for my life in His perfect timing. I have faith. I am a daughter of the King.

*My brethren, count it all **joy** when ye fall into divers temptations; Knowing this, that the trying of your faith worketh **patience**. But let patience have its perfect work, that you may be perfect and entire, **lacking nothing**. James 1:2-4*

*That Christ may dwell in your **hearts** by **faith**; that ye, being rooted and grounded in **love**. Ephesians 3:17*

The closure of my marriage and the process of healing leading to it over the last two years has been supported by God's gentle hand. I am comfortable presently not knowing all of the details as to "Why", "How", or "Should of, could of, would of". I did my best with the tools I had at the time.

Because of God's mercy and grace, I have been able to forgive my ex-husband. Because of God's mercy and grace, I forgive myself. By knowing God more deeply now, I can whole-heartedly trust in His Word that He has amazing things in store for me. I now know that if I keep God in the center of my life, He will protect me and be able to bless me with His great plans.

This includes God being the center of all areas of my life: purpose, career, ministry, relationships, marriage, finances, health, family, ALL areas. Above anything else (or anyone else), I will seek God. I will pick up my cross and walk alongside Him. I will leave my burdens at His feet. *But ye seek first the kingdom of God, and his righteousness; and all these things shall be added unto you. Matthew 6:33. It is better to trust in the Lord than to put confidence in man. Psalms 118:8*

> *It is better to **trust in the Lord** than to put confidence in man. Psalm 118:8*

God has been with me my entire life. I am blessed. But when I really became aware of this, I started to see Him move more in my life and I was able to be an active participant with Him. I began to walk more boldly in confidence knowing that God's hand would show up.

After I left my first lawyer's consultation for my divorce, I decided to meet a friend for coffee at the mall. This day, fittingly, I had a little more "wind beneath my sails". I was suited up in a royal blue blazer, black leather belt, and black leather boots that were made for walking (aka strutting).

I marched down the mall isles intently and I told myself I was there "strictly for business". My focus was suddenly shifted to a six-foot-five tall dapper man with short flowy brown hair and sweet brown eyes. He continued to bless me with an abundance of skin care and self-care options that would soon prove useful in my overall healing journey.

More notably, this gentleman became a friend in Christ as we shared about commonalities in our faith walks. Next, more spiritual family, brothers, sisters, aunts, and uncles, would join the group. It is ultimately God's hope for us to dwell and flourish in a fruitful and robust community. I had prayed for a community of Believers to grow with, and God provided it to me in the most unique and perfect way. God has revealed to me I am His loved daughter, royalty, His princess.

*And he will **love** thee, and **bless** thee, and*
***multiply** thee. Deuteronomy 7:13*

*The Spirit itself beareth witness with our spirit, that we are the **children of God**: And if children, then heirs; heirs of God, and **joint-heirs with Christ**. Romans 8:16-17*

*But the Comforter, which is the **Holy Ghost**, whom the Father will send in my name, he shall teach you all things, and bring all things to your **remembrance**, whatsoever I have said unto you. John 14:26*

MIRACLES AND WONDERS

When God shows up in your life, expect miracles and wonders. I have seen God move tremendously in my recent storms, and I look back and see that He has been with me all of my life. I am reminded of His undeniable power and greatness, for the miracles and wonders He has done in me.

It does not always come as a big surprise or firework show, but instead, steady over time and in His perfect timing and way. To name a few miracles and wonders in review and by no means, to be underestimated: God has blessed me with a beautiful home that serves as a quiet place of healing, security, and growth; God provided me with a safe and reliable vehicle to go out into the community and serve. God blessed me with a wonderful career that brings me great joy, stability, and an outlet to serve the community in a meaningful God-led way. God has provided my finances to meet all of my needs now and in times that I did not see possible.

God granted me with a supportive family, fellow Believers, friends, and a community of hope and love. Through God's provision, my health has been renewed and restored. I am healthier now than I have ever been. I have been made holy and pure in Christ Jesus. I am eternally grateful. And I know this is just the beginning of this Holy ride!

*Who is like unto thee, O Lord, among the gods? Who is like thee, **glorious in holiness**, **fearful in praises**, doing wonders? Exodus 15:11*

*And a **great multitude** followed Him, because they saw His **miracles** which He did on them that were diseased. John 6:2*

Jesus answered them and said, Verily, verily, I say unto you,
*Ye **seek** me, not because ye saw the miracles, but because*
*ye did eat of the loaves, and were **filled.** John 6:26*

John answered, saying unto them all, I indeed baptize you with water; but
one mightier than I cometh, the latchet of whose shoes I am not worthy to
*unloose: he shall baptize you with the **Holy Ghost** and with **fire**. Luke 3:16*

I AM WORTHY

God has provided me with all of my needs. He has shown up in my life in ways that I could have never even imagined. If there is something I am yearning for, I know that God is shaping my heart to become like Him as I trust He is working out every detail in my life for His greater plan. Even though God has given me things (experiences, circumstances, blessings) in ways that I do not completely understand, I know that His ways are best. His ways are creative. His ways are not our ways.

One particular example of God's mystery and magnificence is by Him showing me prophecy. As I learned more about the history of the Lord through scripture and His children in past generations, I understand the numerous gifts of His children. I felt a connection to prophecy early on in my faith journey as well as a calling for more. People with prophetic gifting started showing up in my life with messages to share with me from the Lord.

I learned that I have a calling of ministry on my life and I will speak to women about personal restoration through God's love. I will have a Godly marriage with children that will serve as a testimony of the Lord's power and grace. I will write a book (this book!) to share God's true heart and desires with His children.

I do not know when all of these blessings will come to pass but I trust God will do His work in His perfect timing. God spoke this encouragement to me through His children when I needed it the most. To top it off, God continues to show His love and tender care for me through His children, a sweet family that is growing over time. Thank you, Jesus. You are so generous. I *am* worthy.

*For my **thoughts** are **not your thoughts,** neither are your ways my ways, saith the Lord. Isaiah 55:8*

*__Trust__ in the Lord with all thine heart, and **lean not** unto thine **own understanding**; Proverbs 3:5*

***Believe** in the Lord your God, so shall ye be established; believe **his prophets**, so shall ye prosper. 2 Chronicles 20:20*

FIRM FOUNDATION

T his is it. I have found what I have been looking for. This is peace, contentment, hope, grace, joy, solitude, a deep-knowing: everything *IS* and will be okay. As I walk around my house this morning preparing for the day ahead, I reflect in gratitude and certainty, that this *IS IT.* I have my coffee in hand, topped with oat milk, cinnamon, and nutmeg. The sun is out, the white noise machine sounds in the background. Jock is playing outside. The bluebirds are singing. I went and fetched my laptop from upstairs to set up at the kitchen table, in the fresh morning light, and bask in this most treasured moment in time.

This stillness, the present: God's Presence. In it, breathes gratefulness for what is, what was, and the optimistic expectancy for what is to come. I sit in between a place of contentment and faith. It is the peace in between the guaranteed waves of a storm that make life be what is supposed to be: amazing and miraculous.

When your house is built on a solid foundation, it will remain untethered through all circumstances. *He is like a man which built an house, and digged deep, and laid the foundation on a rock: and when the flood arose, the stream beat vehemently upon that house, and could not shake it: for it was founded upon a rock. Luke 6:48.* When your heart is made pure and perfect through God's reconstruction, blessings will flow from it abundantly and will be received in return.

*For as he thinketh in his **heart**, so is he. Proverbs 23:7*

*Let your **heart** therefore be **perfect** with the Lord our God, to walk in His statutes, and to keep His commandments, as at this day. 1 Kings 8:61*

*Be ye therefore **perfect**, even as your **Father** which is in **heaven** is perfect. Matthew 5:48*

*Behold, I have done according to thy words: lo, I have given thee a **wise** and an **understanding heart**; so that there was none like thee before thee, neither after thee shall any arise like unto thee. 1 Kings 3:12*

THE RAINBOW

In some situations after a storm, we are fortunate if we are blessed with a beautiful rainbow. In my most recent Texas summer storm, a rainbow did not appear. But that is okay! Because unlike temperamental Texas weather, I know God's promises will prevail in my life.

God created the magnificence of a rainbow in which He explains represents an everlasting covenant between Him and every living creature on Earth. That is, God's promise to work all things together for good is the guarantee for your life if you follow His commandments. His commandments? To love your God and to serve Him with all your heart and with all your soul. Number two, love your neighbor as yourself.

For me, it was easy to love God. God loved me first. He came to me in a time of great suffering, physically, emotionally, and spiritually, and surrounded me with His perfect love. Once you get to know a love like this, you can not deny it. True love is reciprocated. You will want to show that love back in return. He has my whole heart.

As you grow to know God, you will grow in His character. Your heart and mind will become like His. You will be a reflection of Christ's image. You will overflow with His unconditional love and share it with others. Your cup will be filled and run over. You will be made brand new and better than before. Life will not necessarily be easy, but the walk in the storm will be significantly more manageable with moments of great joy. You will walk a path of strength and love that is unshakable. This is the promise. A great promise, to be awoken by Jesus.

Most recently, as I ventured out to meet some friends for dinner, a strong and radiant rainbow covered the greater of downtown Austin. A sweet and tender reminder that He'a got us all covered and enveloped in His love, through and through the storms. He is the brilliant author of our Heavenly stories. All glory be to God!

*And the **bow** shall be in the cloud; and I will look upon it, that I may **remember** the everlasting **covenant** between God and every living creature of all flesh that is upon earth. Genesis 9:16*

*Finally, brethren, farewell. Be **perfect,** be of good **comfort,** be of one **mind**, live in **peace**; and the God of **love and peace** shall be with you. 2 Corinthians 13:11*

*And it shall come to pass, if ye shall hearken diligently unto my **commandments** which I command you this day, to **love** the Lord your God and to **serve** Him with all your **heart** and with all your **soul**, Deuteronomy 11:13*

*Beloved, let us **love one another**: for **love** comes from God, and every one that loveth is born of God, and knoweth God. He that loveth not knoweth not God; for **God is love**. 1 John 4:7-8*

The Beatitudes

Blessed *be ye poor:*

for yours is the **kingdom of God***.*

Blessed *are ye that hunger now:*

For ye shall be **filled***.*

Blessed *are ye that weep now,*

For ye shall **laugh***.*

Blessed *are ye, when men shall hate you,*

And when they shall separate you from their company,

and shall reproach you, and cast out your name as evil,

For the **Son of Man's sake***.*

Rejoice *ye in that day, and leap for* **joy***:*

for behold, your **reward** *is great in* **heaven***,*

Luke 6:20-23

ABOUT THE AUTHOR

Olivia Marie Solomon is a joyous and adventurous spirit who is dedicated and excited to share her heart with her readers. Olivia was born in Long Island, New York and earned her Masters in Communication Sciences and Disorders in Central Florida. Olivia's work as a Speech-Language Pathologist across the nation and personal life experiences have embarked her on an amazing journey of self-reflection, faith development, and loving others deeply. Olivia values knowledge and personal growth, and has a roaring passion to encourage others to excel in all areas of their life.

Printed in the United States
by Baker & Taylor Publisher Services